Behold Your MOTHER

Behold Your MOTHER

Learning to Love Mary with the Saints

Peter Kahn

All booklets are published
thanks to the generosity of the supporters
of the Catholic Truth Society

CATHOLIC TRUTH SOCIETY

The bible quotations in this booklet are from the *English Standard Version Catholic Edition*, unless otherwise indicated.

 First published 2023 by The Incorporated Catholic Truth Society, 42-46 Harleyford Road, London SE11 5AY. Tel: 020 7640 0042.
www.ctsbooks.org

ISBN 978 1 78469 756 3

CONTENTS

Foreword

In 1950 when the Venerable Pope Pius XII defined the dogma of Our Lady's Assumption, there was a great deal of enthusiasm in the Catholic world. The devout faithful were jubilant; priests were vying with each other to preach more eloquently on the privileges of our heavenly Mother; and theologians were delving deeper into the writings of the Fathers to discover perhaps still further treasures of grace that Divine Providence might be holding in store for future dogmatic definitions. The titles "Co-Redemptrix" and "Mediatrix of All Grace" were on the lips of many.

Less than two decades later, after the Second Vatican Council, things had changed. When I was young, I can remember an older gentleman telling me of how, one day after the Council, a priest held up a rosary from the pulpit and said: "We don't need this anymore!" Like so many other areas in the life of the Church, Marian devotion was entering a long, dark winter from which it has not yet recovered.

And yet, three centuries ago, St Louis-Marie de Montfort wrote that, as the end of the world draws closer, devotion to Mary should not decrease but rather increase. So, what could possibly explain the sudden drop in devotion to Mary, especially in light of the numerous apparitions in modern times, if not an attempt by the Enemy of human nature to get us away from the one he knows all too well to be as "awesome as an army with banners" (*Sg* 6:10) to him and his followers?

Satan hates Mary, for what he lost through pride, she won through humility. That is why there is an eternal enmity between them which was revealed at the very dawn of history: "I will put enmities between you and the woman...; she will crush your head" (*Douay-Rheims Bible*, *Gn* 3:15). The devil knows his time is running out to take souls to Hell, and so he redoubles his efforts and attacks, giving rise to cruel persecutions and laying snares for the faithful servants and true children of Mary, because he finds them more difficult to overcome than the rest. That is why we must have greater recourse to her, for she it is who leads the servants of Christ to victory.

St Louis-Marie de Montfort also tells us that Our Lady will raise up in the end times saints greater than those of previous times, because in those days, greater saints will be needed to face greater perils to the faith. Where will Mary find those souls if not among those most devoted to her Immaculate Heart and her virtues of humility and purity?

This amazing little book by Peter Kahn encourages us all to ask Our Lady for the grace to become one of those saints.

Let us not be afraid to take up the challenge of promoting her honour and leading souls to her. And should there be anyone infected with that unhealthy fear of taking away from Jesus by praying to Mary, let us reassure them that Jesus is no unnatural Son and that any prayer we make to Mary, any honour we give to her, does not decrease, but rather increases his own glory. Jesus and Mary are one. Let us not separate what God has united.

The author quotes St Maximilian Kolbe as saying: "Never be afraid of loving the Blessed Virgin too much. You can never love her more than Jesus did." St Bernard of Clairvaux had already said, "*De Maria numquam satis*": "Of Mary we can never say enough." All of us would do well to remember those words. As the battle for the Church, which is really a battle for souls, intensifies, let us have ever greater recourse to our Mother, the *Virgo potens* – "Virgin most powerful" – confident that under her immaculate mantle we will take part in the victory.

Dom Pius Mary Noonan, O.S.B.
Notre Dame Priory, Colebrook, Tasmania
12th December 2022
Feast of Our Lady of Guadalupe

Preface

The inspiration for this book stems in part from a comment that Dom Pius Mary Noonan (see the foreword on pages 8-9) made to me many years ago during a retreat which comprised of five days of spiritual exercises. He observed that I had not said much to him about Our Lady in my reflections on my life. His remark stayed with me long after other memories of the retreat faded, influencing my ongoing relationship with Our Lady.

At a certain point I found myself exploring ideas for a possible book. The original inspiration was to write a book that recounted the life of Our Lady, but I found that my subject eluded me. During my explorations, though, I became intrigued by the varied ways that different saints experienced their relationship with Jesus's mother. As noted below, the aim of this book is to help readers come closer to Mary, and thus to live more profoundly with Christ's own life. The book mainly consists of stories from the lives of the saints, stories that tell of ways in which the saints were connected to Mary.

When writing a biography, though, one of the key things an author usually does is to gather testimony from those who had personally known the subject. Mary is not a myth: she is a living person. The saints are those who have known her well. Even if the book does not directly offer a life of Our Lady, an account of the saints' experience of Mary as their mother has a great deal to offer in biographical terms. Mary's incredible tenderness shines through again and again, for instance, as does the utmost care she takes for all her children. She remains ever responsive to her son, Jesus.

I am grateful to all those who have made comments on previous drafts of this book. Thanks also go to my wife and sons for bearing with me while I was busy writing. I have not been able to include details of all the books that have been useful to me in my work on this book, but I am appreciative of the insights of many authors.

PETER KAHN
Palm Sunday, 2023

Such a good friend of ours

Mary, the mother of Jesus, appeared to three young shepherds in Fátima, Portugal, several times during 1917. Lúcia dos Santos and her cousins Francisco and Jacinta Marto saw a vision of a woman brighter than the sun who was clothed in a white shawl edged with gold. The children quickly came to develop a natural rapport with the lady. Once when Lúcia was upset, Jacinta said to the other two, "The Lady will help us always. She's such a good friend of ours!"[1] This closeness to "the Lady", Our Lady, spilled over into a closeness to her son. After one of the apparitions, Lúcia told Francisco that Jesus would join the final apparition. Francisco's response was to say, "Oh, how wonderful! I've only seen Him twice, and I love Him so much!"[2]

It is as if Jesus was a new friend to the three seers. It is no surprise that Francisco and Jacinta have both been

[1] Fr Louis Kondor (Ed.) *Fatima in Lucia's own words* (Secretariado dos Pastorinhos, 2007) p. 50.

[2] *Ibid.*, p. 149.

canonised as saints, while Lúcia's cause is in progress. What would it be like if each of us could experience a similarly deep connection with Mary and Jesus?

Saint Thérèse of Lisieux, meanwhile, came to be close to Mary as a young girl when growing up in late-nineteenth-century France. She once recalled a time when she had visited the church of Our Lady of Victories in Paris. Speaking of Our Lady, she said, "I realised that she watched over me, that I was her child, and so I could not give her any name but *Maman*, because that seemed so much more tender than 'Mother'."[3] St Thérèse had lost her mother as a four-year-old some years earlier. Perhaps the way that St Thérèse came to see Our Lady as her mother was something exceptional – but, then again, perhaps not?

The mother of all Christians

It is, of course, the teaching of the Church that Mary is not only the mother of Jesus but also the mother of all his followers. Even still, it is one thing to hear a statement such as this, but something quite else to live in light of it. If we are to grow into a tender appreciation of Mary as our mother, in our own turn, it will help if we can appreciate that this teaching goes right back to the very beginnings of the Christian faith. This teaching is fundamental to what it means to be a follower of Christ.

---

[3] Fr John Saward, "St Thérèse's Teacher: Our Lady of the Little Way", *Homiletic and Pastoral Review*, 1st October 2011.

In John's Gospel, at the crucifixion, Jesus gave the beloved disciple, St John, to Mary as her son, and he gave Mary to the disciple as his mother:

> When Jesus saw his mother and the disciple whom he loved standing nearby, he said to his mother, "Woman, behold, your son!" Then he said to the disciple, "Behold, your mother!" And from that hour the disciple took her to his own home. (*Jn* 19:26-27)

Jesus spoke first to Mary rather than to the disciple. The effect is to suggest that it is first of all St John who is given to Mary rather than the other way around. Indeed, it is hard to imagine any widow in the entire Bible who was less in need of being consigned to the care of someone outside her family than Mary. Whenever Mary is mentioned in the Gospels, she is present in the company of other family members, whether that of her son, husband, cousin, nephews, sister-in-law or relatives in general. Something other than a desire on Jesus's part to care for his mother must have been going on.

Jesus used the term "woman" to address his mother. Eve is the only other person in the Bible, apart from Mary, who is ever called "Woman". Genesis indicates that Eve was given her name "because she was the mother of all living" (3:20). St John was the first person to notice this parallel that Jesus made between his mother and Eve. It is traditionally understood that St John was the author of the Book of Revelation. We read there that a woman clothed with the sun appeared as a great sign in heaven and that she "gave birth to a male child, one who is to rule all the nations with a rod of iron" (*Rv* 12:5). The scene ends with the dragon going on to "make war on the rest of her offspring, on those who keep the commandments of God and hold to the testimony of Jesus" (*Rv* 12:17). John set up a parallel with Genesis, not only with the reference to a woman, but also by highlighting the enmity between the serpent and the woman and the enmity between the serpent and the offspring of the woman. St John evidently understood that Jesus regarded his mother as the Second Eve, as the mother of all who are brought to life through his redemptive suffering on Calvary.

A living person who loves us

The aim of this book is to help readers come closer to Mary, and thus to live more profoundly with Christ's own life. The book mainly consists of stories from the lives of the saints, stories that tell of ways in which the saints experienced Mary as their mother. It is true, of course, that Mary is one of the saints as well, but she is nonetheless set apart from the rest of the saints as the Mother of God, as the mother of the one who is to rule all the nations.

The book's chapters are framed by scriptural texts that concern Mary's life on earth, and they also integrate within them accounts of the origins of Marian devotions. As well as filling out our understanding of what it means to take Mary as one's mother, consideration of these texts and accounts will allow us to see with clarity that a relationship with Mary is an integral aspect of the Christian faith. Each of the chapters opens a window onto what is entirely possible in the life of any Christian. There is nothing that is more natural in this world than to have a close relationship with one's own mother.

St Maximilian Kolbe was in born in Poland at the end of the nineteenth century. He became a Franciscan friar and was killed in the Auschwitz concentration camp as part of a reprisal for the escape of another inmate. As a devoted apostle of the Virgin Mary, St Maximilian was keenly aware that Our Lady is a person who is alive. He wrote that, with Mary, "one is not coping with an abstract problem to be deciphered, but with a living person who loves us". He similarly once reminded a German official, after an initial period of being confined in an internment camp, that "the Most Holy Virgin Mary is not a fairy tale or a legend, but a living being who loves each one of us". We will see across this book that she finds many ways to be close to all her children.

Hands and feet

In the Holy Trinity fresco, Our Lady both points out St John to the viewer and points towards Jesus on the cross. The fresco provides an invitation to reflection for the viewer, as the scene cannot be taken in all at once. For instance, if you look closely, you can see the feet of God the Father, as if he too, like Mary and John, was standing near to the

cross. The hands of the Father support the weight of the cross. The painting is a study of hands and feet. The Spirit, meanwhile, is present between the Father and the Son in the form of a white dove. Indeed, it seems that the painting was particularly aimed at those who had come into the church to ponder on life and death. The painting is located opposite a door that opens onto a cloistered graveyard; it is what one first sees on entering the church from the cemetery. This book, in its turn, offers the reader an opportunity to reflect on this scene in which Jesus established a relationship between his mother and St John.

The first word comes from God

The earliest account of an apparition of Mary comes from Gregory of Nyssa in 380. He wrote a biography of St Gregory the Wonderworker, who had been born in 213. At that time, visions were primarily conceived of as dreams, so the apparition is described as a "waking vision". Sleep eluded Gregory one night in his worry about the state of the Church. Heresies, truly, were endemic in the early Church. Among the most dangerous of those early heresies was the one taught by Arian. He claimed that Jesus was not God. At its peak, vast swathes of the Church went over to Arianism. St John and Our Lady appeared to Gregory and explained to him what was true. At Our Lady's request, St John handed to Gregory a creed that proclaimed the nature of the Trinity. We are told that Mary appeared with a beauty that was so exceptional that Gregory was unable to look at her in any sustained fashion.

Whatever the historical details of the Wonderworker's life, the notion of Mary appearing to someone was something that Christians of Gregory of Nyssa's day found convincing.

Our Lady is portrayed as reaching out to Gregory the Wonderworker in response to a heartfelt need on his part.

Taking the initiative

A characteristic feature of any apparition of Our Lady, including this one to Gregory, is that she takes the initiative. Whatever one makes of any specific apparition that is claimed to have taken place, the graces that have come into the world through Fátima, Guadalupe, Lourdes and other places have been staggering. The apparitions at Fátima, for instance, have led to a worldwide movement of prayer, while the apparitions at Guadalupe contributed decisively to the conversion of the peoples of South America.

Our Lady's initiative is apparent in the foundation of Mother Teresa's Missionaries of Charity. Our Lady appeared to Mother Teresa – now St Teresa of Calcutta – shortly before the order was founded. Fr Joseph Langford had a long association with Mother Teresa, as the co-founder of the Missionaries of Charity Fathers. He recounts how Mother Teresa once saw a vision of a crowd of people who were both poor and weighed down by intense suffering:

> Our Lady was there in the midst of them, and Mother Teresa was kneeling at her side. Mother Teresa was turned towards the suffering children and so could not see Our Lady's face, but she heard her say: "Take care of them – they are mine. – Bring them to Jesus – carry Jesus to them. – Fear not. – Teach them to say the Rosary – the

family Rosary and all will be well. – Fear not. – Jesus and I will be with you and with your children."[4]

Fr Langford further relates how Mother Teresa received a second vision of the same crowd of poor people:

> This time they were covered in darkness. There, in the midst of an anguished crowd that seemed unaware of his presence, was Jesus on the Cross. Our Lady was before him "at a little distance." Mother Teresa saw herself there as well, not as an adult but "as a little child" standing directly in front of Our Lady as they both faced the cross. Our Lady's left hand was on Mother Teresa's left shoulder, supporting her, and her right hand was holding Mother Teresa's right arm, outstretched towards the crucified Jesus. Jesus then said to her "I have asked you. They have asked you, and she, My mother, has asked you. Will you refuse to do this for me – to take care of them, to bring them to me?"

I am the servant of the Lord

It is clear in Mother Teresa's vision that Jesus's presence underpins the initiative that Mary takes. Pope Benedict XVI wrote that "the first word, the true initiative, the true activity comes from God". The same characteristic form of initiative on God's part is present in the biblical accounts of the creation of the world, the Annunciation and Pentecost.

---

[4] Fr Joseph Langford, *Mother Teresa: In the Shadow of Our Lady* (Our Sunday Visitor, 2007) p. 20.

The words that the angel spoke to Mary, "The Holy Spirit will come upon you, and the power of the Most High will overshadow you" (*Lk* 1:35), evoke the first words of the Bible, where we are told that the Spirit of God "was hovering over the face of the waters" (*Gn* 1:2). In both cases, it is God's word, what God says, that brings life into being. Mary, indeed, says quite explicitly, "Behold, I am the servant of the Lord; let it be to me according to your word" (*Lk* 1:38).

The connection between the accounts of the Annunciation and Pentecost is even stronger, given the use of the terms, "Spirit", "power" and "come upon" in both Luke and the Acts of the Apostles. One of the key features of the account of Pentecost in Acts is that the disciples speak many languages, overcoming the effects of the Fall that were apparent early on in Genesis, at the Tower of Babel, when the Lord "confused the language of all the earth" (*Gn* 11:9). God has brought a new creation into being, by taking the initiative in the life of Mary, the Second Eve.

No marketplaces, paved streets or mosaics

God especially acts in the lives of the lowly. Mary was clearly aware of this in her prayer, the *Magnificat*, in Luke's Gospel (*Lk* 1:46-55). The prayer acknowledges that God had done remarkable things for her, looking on the humble estate of his servant and exalting her. The prayer manifests a keen awareness on the part of Mary of the action of God in her life.

Mary, certainly, was lowly. It has been estimated that Nazareth contained at most 500 people when Mary lived there. The archaeological evidence suggests that the lives of the villagers of Nazareth centred around subsistence farming.[5] As well as working in the fields and raising animals, they would have built their own dwellings, spun their own clothes, preserved food and cared for their children. They would also have paid taxes to the temple authorities in Jerusalem, the Romans and the local Jewish ruler of Galilee. Villagers would have lived together in extended families, each one of these sharing a courtyard, oven, cistern and millstone. There is no evidence of there ever having been any marketplaces, paved streets, mosaics and so on in Nazareth at that time, nor are there any markers of individual affluence, in the form of imported goods, decorated vases or glass objects. By contrast, the nearby historic capital of Galilee, Sepphoris, contained elegant family homes, as well as public buildings, shops, storage facilities, workshops, frescoes, mosaics and sewage channels – a different world from that inhabited by Mary when the angel Gabriel appeared to her.

St Thérèse of Lisieux is especially articulate about Our Lady's humility at the Annunciation in a poem called "Why I love you, O Mary!" that she wrote in 1897 as she lay dying:

> When an angel from Heaven bids you be the Mother
> Of God who is to reign for all eternity,

---

5 Jonathan Reed, *Archaeology and the Galilean Jesus* (Bloomsbury, 2002).

I see you prefer, O Mary, what a mystery!
the ineffable treasure of virginity.

The poem suggests that Mary preferred to be a virgin rather than to become the Mother of God. The implication is that it was such lowliness on Mary's part that led the Son of God to choose Mary as his mother. Thérèse herself had longed to embark on the life of a consecrated virgin early in life – so deeply, in fact, that she became a Carmelite sister when she was fifteen years old.

How can the ark of the Lord come to me?

After God had acted in her life at the Annunciation, Mary made haste to visit her cousin Elizabeth, who had in her old age conceived a son. Luke's account of the Visitation emphasises that it is as if Elizabeth had received a visit from God present in the Ark of the Covenant. Commentators have pointed out that there is a close connection between Luke's description of the Visitation and the arrival of the Ark of the Covenant in Jerusalem under King David. The same word "leap" is used to describe both the way that David reacted with joy at the arrival of the ark and the response of John the Baptist in his mother's womb to Christ's arrival. The wonder that Elizabeth expressed at Mary's coming to visit her – "Why is this granted to me that the mother of my Lord should come to me?" (*Lk* 1:43) – is mirrored in the fear that David had earlier expressed at the possibility that the ark might come into his house: "How can the ark of the Lord come to me?" (*2 S* 6:9). As the Mother of God, Our Lady's initiative in the lives of others is now closely joined to God's initiative in their lives as well.

An unforgettable thing

It is the experience of the saints that Mary has continued to take the initiative over the centuries in ways that are full of motherly attention. Our Lady appeared to the peasant St Juan Diego in 1531 in Mexico. While an age of time separates us from the actual events themselves, a contemporary account called the *Nican mopohua* preserved details of the apparition. After mentioning that St Juan was drawn to the top of a hill called Tepeyac by the sound of many precious birds, the account records the first apparition of Our Lady to Juan as follows:

> And then when the singing suddenly stopped, when it could no longer be heard, he heard someone calling him from the top of the hill, someone was saying to him: "Dear Juan, dearest Juan Diego."[6]

The tenderness of Mary's greeting to him in the local language is astounding: "*Juantzin, Juan Diegotzin*." The ending "*zin*" is usually rendered as "dear", but this does not do justice to the sense of affection and intimacy that it conveys. Our Lady subsequently referred to Juan as her

---

6 Carl A. Anderson and Eduardo Chavez, *Our Lady of Guadalupe: Mother of the Civilization of Love* (Penguin Random House, 2009) p. 173.

"dearest and youngest son", even though he was over fifty at the time of the apparitions. She went on to refer to herself as Juan's "dear mother" (*inantzin*) and as a "compassionate mother" (*nohuacanantzin*). Juan's uncle was close to death when Mary appeared to Juan for a fourth time. Juan asked for permission to break off from the apparition to go to call a priest to hear his uncle's confession and prepare him for his death. Our Lady's response was to say to Juan that his uncle had already been healed and that there was no need for Juan to be worried or to grieve over his uncle's illness. Our Lady anticipated Juan's request with her own motherly care for his uncle.

Furthermore, Christ's presence was subtly present in the apparitions to St Juan. Our Lady asked Juan to convey a request to the local bishop for a church to be built on the hill of the apparitions. To convince the bishop to honour the request, an image of Our Lady was miraculously imprinted onto Juan's tilma. In the image you can see a purple ribbon tied high above the waist. At the time in Mexico, such a belt was only worn in this position by pregnant women. Mary awaits the birth of her Son in this image. As Our Lady of Guadalupe, Mary had a message of mercy for the peoples of South America. She pointed to the value of human life in the womb, even while child sacrifice was still clandestinely practised across Mexico.

Conclusion

It is, of course, an integral aspect of being a mother to take the initiative in the lives of one's children. As a boy, Christ learned to pray beside his mother. Forty days after he was born, Mary and Joseph brought Jesus to the temple to offer sacrifices to the Lord. We are told that Jesus's parents "went to Jerusalem every year at the Feast of the Passover" (*Lk* 2:41) and that when Jesus was twelve years old he went with them. What faithful son or daughter does not go on to respond to his or her mother's initiative? Jesus went up again and again to Jerusalem for the feast of Passover, testifying through his own life to his mother's wisdom. Before he went up to Jerusalem for the last time, the people said to one another "What do you think? That he will not come to the feast?" (*Jn* 11:56) It was clear to all that if he joined the festival, he would be arrested by the chief priests and killed. Even in the face of death, Jesus went up to Jerusalem one last time for the feast. Our Lady's motherly attention calls for a response from us, just as it did from Jesus. It is to our response that we now turn.

Call me blessed

The origins of devotion to Mary quite evidently started with Jesus himself. The Gospel of Luke tells us that Jesus was submissive to Mary and to her husband Joseph (*Lk* 2:51). Jesus fulfilled the commandment of the Law to honour his father and mother. The Hebrew word for "honour" in this commandment, *kabed*, is used elsewhere in the Bible in reference to glorifying others. To point out the blessings that someone else has received is to honour that person. Jesus thus both obeyed his mother and paid her honour. As a result, there is every reason for me to pay honour to the mother of Christ and to praise her. At least, this is the case if I no longer live, but Christ lives in me, as St Paul writes in Galatians (2:20).

Across all generations

After Elizabeth had expressed wonder at her cousin's visit, the Gospel account relates that she called Mary "blessed". Elizabeth exclaimed with a loud cry, "Blessed are you among women, and blessed is the fruit of your womb!" (*Lk* 1:42).

Before he became Pope Benedict XVI, Joseph Ratzinger noted in his book *Daughter Zion* that by incorporating the phrase "For behold, from now on all generations will call me blessed" within the *Magnificat*, Luke knew that the Church of his day praised Mary and that this praise would continue for all time. Luke thus saw devotion to Mary as a core feature of Christian practice.

Ever since the earliest days, Christians have continued to find ways to call Mary blessed. For instance, there is only a modest gap in time between the writing of the last books of the New Testament and the writing of a book called the *Protoevangelium of James*. This second-century text recounts the early life of Mary, from her own conception to the birth of her son. Scholars are generally agreed that the main aim of this text was to praise the Virgin Mary, even if much of the detail seems fabricated. Joseph was apparently chosen as a husband for Mary after a dove flew forth from his rod!

Why would God give a commission to the Church, across all generations, to call Mary blessed? To some it seems out of place to lavish attention on her – as if she had done her job in giving birth to Christ and then should be forgotten for evermore. One answer to this question is that in praising her as far as one is able one soon realises that one cannot do her glories justice, because God's action is far greater than we can ever appreciate. We see this even in Elizabeth's greeting to Mary. It was not sufficient for Elizabeth to stop at calling Mary blessed. A recognition of the blessings that Mary had received from God naturally led on to a recognition of the blessings that came through the fruit of her womb, Jesus.

Growth in prayer

What is evident is that attempting to glorify Mary leads one to ponder on what God has done for his lowly servant. In seeking to find ways to call Mary blessed, the saints mused upon her life and upon the life of her Son. Acquiring a taste for meditation might seem exotic, but the readiness to find meaning in words or images is a truly basic feature of the Christian life. In her classic work, *The Interior Castle*, St Teresa of Avila compared the soul to a castle in which there were many apartments or mansions. This work portrays what it takes to grow into the depths of sanctity through ever-more-intense forms of prayer. In the centre of the soul is the innermost set of mansions where the King dwells. St Teresa understood meditation to involve attempts at understanding that attach meaning to the words you utter:

> As far as I can understand, the door of entry into this castle, and thus to the first or the outermost mansion, is prayer and meditation: I do not say mental prayer rather than vocal, for, if it is prayer at all, it must be accompanied by meditation. If a person does not think Whom he is addressing, and what he is asking for, and who it is that is asking and of Whom he is asking it, I do not consider that he is praying at all even though he be constantly moving his lips.

Mary was herself given over to meditation as part of the fabric of her prayer. Our Lady's prayer, the *Magnificat*, itself constitutes a meditation on a series of Old Testament texts. The prayer primarily consists of an adaptation of the prayer that Hannah, the mother of the prophet Samuel, prayed in 1 Samuel 2, but it is possible to identify at least sixteen allusions to separate parts of the Old Testament in this short prayer of Our Lady! It would not have been possible for Mary to have prayed this prayer without partly attending to these resonances. It is intriguing that the *Our Father* also incorporates within it echoes of Old Testament passages. Pope Benedict XVI once pointed out that Jesus had his mother to thank for his human self-consciousness. Learning to meditate on God's actions is a foundational aspect of prayer. To pray in this way is to hold on to the testimony of Jesus.

Pray the Rosary!

The Rosary provides a wonderful example of praise of Our Lady that leads straight to meditation. The Rosary entails a series of prayers that are said one after the other, including the *Hail Mary*, the *Our Father* and the *Glory Be*. In praying the *Hail Mary* many times over, Mary's praises sound out again and again. While the Rosary has been known in various forms since the ninth century, the form which it currently takes is the one that, according to tradition, was established by St Dominic in the thirteenth century, after

Our Lady appeared to him. It became common to meditate on different incidents in the life of Christ (and his mother) as part of the prayer from the fifteenth century onwards. One meditates on a mystery such as the Incarnation or the Annunciation, while praying the *Our Father* once, the *Hail Mary* ten times and the *Glory Be* once. It was found that the regular rhythm of the prayer lent itself to a stillness that supports meditation. Through praying the Rosary we learn to meditate, and we thereby grow into the very first stage of prayer.

Many saints grew attached to praying the Rosary as young children, taking Mary into the heart of their lives. St Louis-Marie de Montfort was born in France during the seventeenth century. Not content, as a young boy, with praying the Rosary, he taught his younger brothers and sisters, and his classmates at school, to do the same. After his ordination as a priest, he became a wandering missionary, spreading devotion to Our Lady as part of parish missions.

St Bernadette Soubirous learnt to pray the Rosary as a young girl, just like others around her in nineteenth-century France. It took her some time to master the prayer, and it seems that she only acquired a set of rosary beads of her own after Our Lady appeared to her at Massabielle, near to the village of Lourdes. Once she did acquire the beads, though, they never left her person.

St Thérèse also became attached to the Rosary as a young girl. She recounted in her autobiography, *The Story of a Soul*, that after making her first confession she asked the priest to bless her Rosary:

> It was evening, and as soon as I got to a street-lamp I stopped and took the newly blessed Rosary out of my pocket, turning it over and over. "What are you looking at, Thérèse, dear?" asked Pauline. "I am seeing what a blessed Rosary looks like." This childish answer amused my sisters very much.

A commentary on the *Hail Mary*

Instead of pondering on a given mystery that relates to Christ's life, one can alternatively take the words of the prayers that make up the Rosary as a focus for meditation. It is worth seeing how this plays out in the initial part of the *Hail Mary*: "Hail Mary, full of grace, the Lord is with thee. Blessed art though amongst women and blessed is the fruit of thy womb, Jesus." This section of the prayer first came into usage during the eleventh century, as part of the Little Office of the Blessed Virgin that monks and nuns said alongside the Church's formal daily pattern of prayers, the *Divine Office*. It provides plenty of subject matter for meditation.

There are many biblical resonances that provide a backdrop for the greeting of the angel Gabriel. Several passages in the Old Testament refer to "Daughter Zion", a personification of the people of Israel. For instance, the prophet Zephaniah told the daughter of Zion: "Rejoice and exult with all your heart" (*Zp* 3:14) and "The King of Israel, the Lord, is in your midst" (*Zp* 3:15). When the Hebrew word that translates as "in your midst" is applied to a woman, it means "in your womb". The second-century theologian Origen of Alexandria noted that no one other than Mary is addressed in the Scriptures with the greeting "Rejoice, O full of grace". This greeting is reserved for Mary alone, indicating that she possessed a unique grace. Rather than the traditional translation "full of grace", though, more recent scholarship suggests that the best translation of this phrase is "you who have been transformed by grace", reflecting, as this does, the sense of prior causation that is present in the Greek. Fr Aidan Nichols argues in *There Is No Rose*[7] that the angel told Mary to rejoice because she already possessed a unique grace, even before Jesus had been conceived. God gave this grace to Mary so that her womb would bear fruit, in Jesus.

The words of Elizabeth, meanwhile, recall the words of the judge in Israel, Deborah, who called Jael "most blessed of women" after Jael killed the commander of a Canaanite army. And a similar blessing was accorded to Judith in the account of her victory over the Assyrian commander, Holofernes, after cutting off his head. When praying the *Hail Mary*, there is every reason to be confident of sharing in a victory over one's enemies, including death.

---

[7] Fr Aidan Nichols, OP, *There Is No Rose: The Mariology of the Catholic Church* (Fortress Press, 2015).

The name of Jesus has been described as a hinge that joins together the two parts of the *Hail Mary*, so that the prayer as a whole focuses on Jesus. When the prayer is said in Latin, the word "Jesus" occurs right in the middle, as the sixteenth out of thirty-one words! The second part of the *Hail Mary*, of course, constitutes a prayer for her intercession, as we shall shortly further explore.

What do you want of me?

As a mother who gives birth to her children, Mary personally leads us to growth in the Christian life through encouraging us to pray the Rosary. When Our Lady appeared to the three seers of Fátima on 13th June 1917, Lúcia asked her, "What do you want of me?" Our Lady's response was to say, "I wish you to come here on the thirteenth of next month, to pray the Rosary every day, and to learn to read." Our Lady repeatedly asked the three seers to pray the Rosary each day. The "Five First Saturdays" represents an associated set of practices that Our Lady requested that Lúcia promote. For five consecutive months, on the first Saturday of the month, one is asked to make a confession, receive Holy Communion, pray the Rosary and meditate for a further fifteen minutes on one of the mysteries of the Rosary. Our Lady promised that those who fulfil this practice will be assured of their salvation, provided they are also committed to self-denial and to the avoidance of sin. This practice offers an explicit encouragement for Christians to engage in meditation. Sanctity does not simply appear by chance: it has its sources.

Who is the Queen of Heaven?

Is there any young child who does not think that his or her mother is the most wonderful person in the world? It is entirely natural for children to speak highly of their mothers. St Thérèse of Lisieux was adept at speaking of Mary in glowing terms. On one occasion she suggested that she was happier than the Mother of God, since she had the Blessed Virgin for her mother, whereas Mary had no such mother to love. The final prayer that St Thérèse wrote before she died was to Our Lady. In this prayer, Thérèse said that, were she to have been the Queen of Heaven and Mary to have been Thérèse, she would have wanted to swap with her so that Mary could be Queen of Heaven all the same.

Calling Mary blessed constitutes a natural response to one's heavenly mother. If the mother is the one who takes the initiative in the life of her child, then it is the task of the child to respond by showing honour and affection. This response carries great grace with it. After all, the commandment of the Law to honour one's father and mother is accompanied by a blessing for those who fulfil it: "...that your days may be long in the land that the Lord your God is giving you" (*Ex* 20:12). The saints show us that calling Mary blessed leads directly to growth in prayer. We shall see in the chapters that follow that the possibilities for this growth are truly astounding. What we do not want to see, though, is any parallel between our own response to Mary and the disdain that David's wife, Michal, expressed at seeing him dance before the Ark of the Covenant in what is imagined to be a loincloth. One can respond to Mary by leaping or crying out with joy – or by being filled with contempt for those who show her heartfelt devotion.

Asking for her assistance

After she had been a Carmelite nun for several years, St Thérèse of Lisieux was given the task of writing her autobiography. At the start of the book, St Thérèse recalls that she set about her duty by kneeling before a statue of Our Lady. The statue had come to the convent from her own family. She had received many proofs of her heavenly mother's loving care before this statue. Indeed, St Thérèse and her earthly mother had each experienced an occasion when the statue seemed to come to life. At the start of her writing, she begged her dear Mother Mary to "guide my hand, and thus ensure that only what was pleasing to her should find place here". St Thérèse had, by then, become accustomed to always looking towards Our Lady in every want that she experienced. For instance, according to one of her sisters, she would at times, prior to receiving Holy Communion, imagine that she was three years old, with ruffled hair and a dirtied smock. She had explained that all that was required was a little attention from Our Lady, who would make her presentable, arrange her hair and present her with a ribbon or a flower – then she would be ready to sit down at the banquet of angels.

Any experience of a lack of something was an occasion for St Thérèse to give expression to her "Little Way", by which she accepted her own insignificance and made sacrifices as an integral aspect of daily life. Thérèse was keenly aware that Our Lady was well placed to provide for her at any given time. Each one of us needs help from God, whether to convert from a life of sin, in the face of personal difficulties, in our attempts to help others or when oppressed by enemies of whatever kind. When God provides our necessities through Mary's hands, then we become more affectionate towards our spiritual mother, and our trust in God grows. To ask for help from Mary is, in its own way, to call her blessed, because we recognise in making the request that she has blessings to share with us.

Deliver us from dangers

As the mother of Christ, the King, Our Lady is able to meet our needs. The Davidic kings of Israel accepted requests that came to them through their mothers. One of the functions of the Queen Mother in ancient Israel was to present to the king requests from the people. In 1 Kings 2, we see Adonijah come to Bathsheba, King Solomon's mother. He was confident that the king would grant his request if Bathsheba were to forward it on. Adonijah said to her, "He will not refuse you." When Elizabeth addressed Mary as "the mother of my Lord" (*Lk* 1:43), she connected directly with these traditions of the Israelite royal court, given that the phrase "my Lord" was used to address royalty.

It is no wonder that we see Jesus honouring a request from his mother in John's Gospel. In response to his mother pointing out that the wedding party had run out of wine, Jesus answered, "Woman, what does this have to do with me? My hour has not yet come" (*Jn* 2:4). In saying this, Jesus implied that the hour would come when he would honour all his mother's requests. Even so, Jesus still honoured this more immediate request.

It did not take long for this biblical tradition to manifest itself in the life of the Church. The earliest known prayer for the intercession of Our Lady is the *Sub Tuum Praesidium*: "We fly to thy patronage, O holy Mother of God; despise not our petitions in our necessities, but deliver us from all dangers, O glorious and blessed Virgin." A copy of this prayer was found in Egypt on a fragment of parchment. It has been dated to the third century on the basis of analysis of historic writing. The prayer's use of the first-person plural suggests a communal setting for its recitation. Only one side of the papyrus, though, contains writing, which suggests that the copy was used as part of a popular devotion rather than within a liturgy. The first part of the prayer acknowledges the graces that God granted to Mary. Calling her blessed in this way makes it possible to seek God's help through her, so that we, too, can grow in charity and share in the transformative

grace that she received. In this way, we too receive blessings from God.

One hand shot, and another guided the bullet

Who is there who does not experience an intense sense of helplessness at times and the need to call out to God for assistance? We can expect Our Lady to hear our prayers, partly because of the depths of her own suffering. A sword pierced her heart at the foot of the cross. Mary is close to us in our trials.

In his spiritual diaries entry for a meditation on 3rd November 1962, Pope St John Paul II indicated that he felt himself very much in Mary's hands and close to God in relation to two specific issues. He did not name the two issues in his diary, but he did wonder whether he was using such feelings for his own ends. He realised, though, that God was using these two issues to assist in his redemption, so that he would convert and give himself over completely to God by turning to Our Lady.

It was well that John Paul had learned to turn to Our Lady in times of difficulty. An assailant shot him multiple times in the abdomen when he entered St Peter's Square for an audience in 1981. His private secretary, Stanislaw Dziwisz, recalled that in the ambulance afterwards, eyes closed and in great pain, John Paul kept on praying, "Mary, my mother!" The assassination attempt occurred on 13th May, the anniversary of the first of the apparitions in Fátima.

It is well known that John Paul attributed his survival to the intercession of his heavenly mother. He said, "One hand shot, and another guided the bullet." He visited Fátima exactly a year later to thank Our Lady for her intervention in his life.

Red from the blows

St Maximilian Kolbe similarly took trials that he experienced as opportunities to come close to the Immaculata. The German authorities closed Maximilian's monastery in 1941, a little while after the invasion of Poland. The Gestapo, the German secret state police, subsequently arrested him and confined him to a prison, before transferring him to Auschwitz. The guards in Auschwitz regularly beat him, given that he continued with his priestly ministry. On one occasion, a sergeant tore Maximilian's rosary beads away from him. The sergeant shoved the crucifix on the rosary towards him and asked if he believed in it. When Maximilian responded "Yes", the sergeant struck him in the face. This routine was repeated several times in a row. When the sergeant moved on, Maximilian's compatriots tried to comfort him. Maximilian, however, said that the whole thing was of no consequence and that they should not be concerned for him. He said that he had borne with the insults simply for love of Mary. He then just continued with his prayers. The witnesses would not have known that anything at all had happened, except that his face was still red from the blows.

Is it any surprise that in the face of oppression from others Maximilian would turn to the woman who – when we remember how in 1 Samuel the presence of the Ark repeatedly brought victory to the Israelites over their Philistine enemies – was the new Ark of the Covenant? It is reported that the final prayer on the lips of St Maximilian as he was killed in Auschwitz was the *Hail Mary*.

The second part of this prayer, of course, runs as follows: "Holy Mary, mother of God, pray for us sinners now and at the hour of our death." This part of the *Hail Mary* first appeared in print at the end of the fifteenth century. The first part of the *Hail Mary* opens up a sense of wonder and certainty at God's action in Mary's life, preparing us for the second part of the prayer, in which we seek God's assistance in the needs that we experience in each present moment and in anticipation of our death.

A lifetime of closeness to Mary similarly enabled St Bernadette to seek Our Lady's assistance on her deathbed. One night as she lay seriously ill, Bernadette asked a specific sister to help her call on Our Lady at the hour of her death. The next day, Bernadette held out her arms to the sister and fixed her eyes on her, but the sister did not understand what she meant by these signs. Bernadette's last words were to say to this sister, "For you to help me." The sister then recalled what she had agreed with Bernadette and led those at the bedside in a prayer of thanksgiving to Our Lady. St Bernadette died almost immediately after this prayer.

Jesus always triumphs

There are, however, countless examples of the saints turning to Our Lady in more mundane settings as well. St Thérèse was appointed the assistant novice mistress for her monastery in 1893, even before she had formally left the novitiate herself. She met her four novices every day for half an hour from 2.30 p.m. until 3 p.m. If she ever found herself making a misstep in her advice to them – perhaps toning down some truth that her novices needed to hear – she indicated how "at once I have recourse to prayer, I turn to Our Blessed Lady, and Jesus always triumphs."[8] To the novices themselves, it seemed as if St Thérèse was able to read their innermost thoughts. In response to a query about this from her novices, she replied:

> Here is my secret. I never make remarks to you before I have invoked the Blessed Virgin. I ask her to inspire me with what will do you the most good. Often I myself am astonished at the things I teach you. In telling you these things, I feel simply that I am not mistaken, and that Jesus speaks through me.[9]

Experience taught her that prayer was far more effective in touching someone else's heart than mere words. What would it mean if each one of us was able to find a way to

---

[8] Fr Emile Neubert, *Life of Union with Mary* (Academy of the Immaculate, 2013) p. 199.

[9] *Ibid.*, p. 170.

turn to Mary in the face of the challenges that we encounter each day?

The old man was strangely grateful

The saints, of course, felt the needs of others as keenly as their own needs. A readiness to pray for others was part of the fabric of Mother Teresa's entire life. She left the religious order that she had joined as a young woman, the Loreto Sisters, when she was thirty-seven years old. She went to serve the poor in the slums of Calcutta, and subsequently recounted her first day on the streets:

> The people were pleased – but the children were all over the place. And what dirt and misery, what poverty and suffering. I spoke very, very little, I just did some washing of sores, and dressings, gave medicine to some. The old man lying on the street – not wanted – all alone just sick and dying. I gave him carborsone and water to drink and the old man was so strangely grateful.[10]

She realised, though, that she could do little in the face of the distresses she encountered without others to help her. She soon found herself at the edge of her own limits to cope, and turned to Our Lady:

> I keep on telling her "I have no children" – just as many years ago she told Jesus "They have no wine." I put all

---

[10] Fr Brian Kolodiejchuk (ed.), *Mother Teresa: Come Be My Light* (Rider, 2008) p. 132.

> my trust in her Heart. She is sure to give me in her own way.[11]

It did not take long for Our Lady to answer her prayers. Within a year of starting her work in Calcutta, Mother Teresa had been joined by a small group of young women. The sense that her work with the poorest of the poor was a gift to her from Our Lady was something that never left her. She almost always held a set of rosary beads in her hands, even when physically caring for someone's pains. People would ask her why she held onto the beads when she was obviously not praying them. In response, she said it was a way of holding onto Our Lady's hand, as her child. The Virgin Mary was a familiar companion to Mother Teresa.

Never refused a grace

Mother Teresa particularly loved the *Memorare* prayer. This is the prayer that starts: "Remember, O most loving Virgin Mary, that it is a thing unheard of that anyone who had recourse to your protection, implored your help, or sought your intercession, was left forsaken." It is a prayer that displays an intense confidence that Our Lady will help us. When she encountered someone facing a difficulty, Mother Teresa would often pray the *Memorare* nine times in a row to beg for God's mercy (a novena) and then a final time to express gratitude for God's answer. This prayer is

---

[11] *Ibid.*, p. 135.

called the flying novena, because it is typically prayed in times of urgent need. The next time you deeply feel a lack of something, why not pray a flying novena?

Mother Teresa once had to secure a visa for a sister in order to replace a superior who had become sick. In communist East Germany at the time, the standard wait for a visa was six months. Mother Teresa began to pray a flying novena for the visa, but before the novena was concluded, a communist official rang to confirm the six-month wait. Mother Teresa decided to pray the novena again, and the phone rang once more. Another official let her know that she would be able to get the visa immediately. It is said that Mother Teresa's requests to Christ through Our Lady were never refused.

Padre Pio, St Pio of Pietrelcina, was a Franciscan friar in the twentieth century who lived in Italy and who bore the wounds of Christ on his hands, feet and side for many years. He once noted, "Our Lady never refuses me a grace through the recitation of the Rosary." The saints show us a way forward, in connecting devotion to Mary with the claims of charity to others. How we should learn from their confidence!

The Miraculous Medal

We also see the saints opening up means by which others can call out to Mary for their own necessities. A simple example of encouraging others to seek Our Lady's help comes in a letter that St Louis-Marie de Montfort wrote to his parents when he was about twenty years old:

> Inform my brother Joseph that I implore him to study diligently so that he will become one of the finest in his class. Let him know that to accomplish this he must strive after the assistance of the Blessed Virgin, his good mother. If he does not cease to display devotion to her, she will provide whatever he needs. I urge my sisters to act likewise.

More dramatically, Our Lady appeared several times in Paris during 1830 to a young novice, St Catherine Labouré. During the second apparition, Mary asked Catherine to have a medal struck upon the model that she showed to her, and to have it distributed. All who wore the medal and repeated the prayer "O Mary conceived without sin, pray for us who have recourse to Thee" were to come under the protection of the Mother of God and to receive abundant graces. An image of Our Lady along with the words of the prayer around the edge is printed on the front of the medal. The back of the medal displays a letter "M" for Mary, intertwined with a cross, above an image of the heart of Mary and that of the Sacred Heart of Jesus. Our Lady spoke to Catherine of how generous she always was towards those who sought her intercession.

A similar promise was made by Our Lady to the Carmelite friar St Simon Stock in Aylesford, England, during an apparition in the thirteenth century. She made an astounding promise to him, that anyone who died wearing the brown scapular from the Carmelite habit would not suffer eternal fire.

The choice to wear a medal or a scapular in honour of Our Lady might seem to be an insignificant act, but if Christ has chosen to open specific avenues by which his mother is able to bring assistance to those who lack something, why should we deny them those paths of grace? Indeed, there is now a long history of miracles and graces that have come upon those who have taken to wearing the medal or the scapular. But what graces St Catherine herself received from the Blessed Virgin Mary after the visions! She subsequently spent forty years of her life on a farm taking care of a group of retired old men – cooking for them, washing their clothes, supporting their leisure activities, taking care of them while sick and praying at their deathbeds. St Catherine's identity as the recipient of the visions in 1830 was only openly revealed after her death.

Now you will be my mother!

Requests for Mary's assistance are closely aligned with the act of calling her blessed. Hand over the challenges that you face during the day to your heavenly mother by praying for her help! The saints often reached out to Our Lady when facing specific needs. It was in this way that they were able to develop a close bond with their dearest mother.

Saint Catherine Labouré, for instance, took Mary to be her mother, after losing her own mother as a nine-year-old. Shortly after her mother's death, a servant to the family saw her climb onto a chair and take down a statue of Our Lady from a shelf. She gave the statue a hug, saying, "Dear Blessed Mother, now you will be my mother!" This deep affection for Mary was linked to an awareness of her own need for a mother. For the saints, prayer to Our Lady involved far more than repeating the words of prayers in a detached fashion.

Pondering on the events of life

Mother Teresa developed a habit of pondering on things that occurred to her during the day. In his book *Mother Teresa: In the Shadow of Our Lady*, Fr Joseph Langford describes how every night Mother Teresa undertook a practice called an examen. Before she retired, Mother Teresa would take time to think of five or so gifts that she had been given that day. This was followed by seeking to discern five occasions when she had been invited to give of herself to others. She thanked God for the occasions when she had welcomed his graces, and asked forgiveness for those times when grace had been spurned.

This examen directly mirrors Mary's practice of pondering on events as they happened to her. We have already seen that Our Lady meditated on the angel Gabriel's greeting to her. In Luke's Gospel, meanwhile, we read that after the birth of Christ, Mary "treasured up" all the things that had occurred to her and "pondered them in her heart" (*Lk* 2:19). The word translated as "ponder" means to cast one beside another, suggesting that Mary reflected on incidents as they occurred to her, trying to make sense of them in relation to each other. The word used for "treasure" in the Greek, furthermore, connects to various passages in the Old Testament, including one in which Jacob treasured up the dream that his son Joseph had received of the sun, the moon and eleven stars bowing down. Jacob sought to understand the meaning of the dream and God's purposes for his son.

Almost every icon or painting that you see of Our Lady indicates that her gaze is within, with her eyes on God. This is the case, for instance, in the image of the Madonna and Child from the Book of Kells, an illuminated manuscript containing the four Gospels. Timothy Verdon in *Mary in Western Art* indicates that there is a close similarity between this page from the Book of Kells and what is probably the very first image of Our Lady, a mother with child portrayed on the wall of the Catacomb of Priscilla in Rome. The wall painting in the catacomb dates from the late-second to the early-third centuries. It seems to have set the scene for depictions of Mary that followed in later centuries.

Many of the gifts and invitations that Mother Teresa called to mind in her nightly examen would already have been linked to Mary's assistance in her life, especially through answered prayers. A readiness to call on Mary's help in times of need supports an awareness of what God is doing in one's life. Furthermore, undertaking the examen enabled Mother Teresa to share in Mary's own way of life. In

doing this, she quite evidently honoured Mary by following her example – and thus, in a way, called her blessed.

Beloved Mama, do not worry for me

Through the happenings they experienced, the saints were keenly aware that God's power was at work. St Maximilian, for instance, established a vast friary at Niepokalanów, Poland. The friary supported a publishing empire, at its height producing a daily newspaper with a circulation of one million copies and a monthly magazine with a circulation of 600,000. When the invading German army dispersed the friars from Niepokalanów, Maximilian reminded his brothers how many souls, as a result, would have occasion to thank the Immaculata for their encountering a friar. During one period of confinement, prior to being sent to the concentration camp at Auschwitz, he told other prisoners who were tempted to plot ridiculous acts of self-defence, "You have no reason to be so annoyed.... This is a trifle, it is all for our Loving Mother."

The most moving letter that Maximilian ever wrote is one final letter to his mother, Maria Kolbe, written in Auschwitz on 15th June 1941.

> My Beloved Mother,
>
> Towards the end of May I came by a train to the Auschwitz camp (in Oświęcim). All is well with me. Beloved Mama, do not worry for me and for my health, because the good God is in every place and with great love He thinks about

> everyone and everything. It would be best not to write to me before I send you another letter, because I do not know how long I will remain here. With warm greetings and kisses, Kolbe Rajmund.[12]

The suffering that Maximilian experienced in Auschwitz was a reminder for him of the goodness and great love of God. If we undertake Mother Teresa's examen each day, then there is every reason to expect that we, too, will be able to perceive how Mary is close to us in the events of our lives.

Singing hymns together

It is intriguing that St Teresa of Avila singled out a capacity to recognise when God is at work in one's life as a distinctive mark of those who have entered the second set of mansions of the interior castle. She wrote that people who live in the second mansions are those who have begun to hear the Lord calling out to them through events in their lives – the conversations of good people, sicknesses and trials, insights in prayer, and so on. Many of the saints, for instance, found that they began to hear God's call more strongly when they joined associations that were centred around devotion to Our Lady. St Thérèse of Lisieux joined the Confrérie du Rosaire de la Très Sainte Vierge when she was eleven years old. The association recited the Rosary together every week and held a Mass for members who had died. She begged

---

[12] St Maximilian Maria Kolbe, *The Writings of St Maximilian Maria Kolbe: Volume I – Letters* (Nerbini International, 2017) Letter 961.

permission from her father to join this association, even though she had no close friends who were already members.

Pope John Paul II – Karol, as he was then called – led the school branch of a similar association from the age of sixteen to the age of eighteen. He went on to join the Living Rosary movement founded by a saintly tailor, Jan Tyranowski. The Gestapo had rounded up a group of Salesian priests in Krakow in 1941. Before being taken away, the priests had asked Jan to continue their work of forming young people. He gathered young men in groups of fifteen, providing group leaders with formation in spirituality and apostolic life. Tyranowski asked Karol to lead one of these groups, introducing him to teaching on contemplative prayer and to the importance of undertaking an examination of one's conscience each day. Tyranowski helped Karol to discern that God was calling him to the priesthood.

Other saints took care to found associations that were dedicated to Our Lady. St Louis-Marie de Montfort's main ministry was to preach missions in parishes. As well as introducing the Rosary, he formed various kinds of lay associations. One of these, for instance, called themselves 'The Penitents'. St Louis-Marie arranged for the thirty-three first members of this association to make a pilgrimage to another city seventy miles away, alternately praying the Rosary and walking in silence as they went. St Louis-Marie had the penitents take off their shoes and sing hymns to Mary for the entry into the city.

Shadows that hide the power of God

Alongside Mary's readiness to ponder on ways that God was at work in her life, we see that she accepted what God had in store for her. Her immediate response to the message from the angel Gabriel that she would conceive in her womb and bear a son was to say, "Behold, I am the servant of the Lord; let it be to me according to your word." Across a large part of the infancy narrative in Luke's Gospel, furthermore, we see that she was obedient to the Law of Moses (*Lk* 2). She did what was required of her by the Law of Moses and went up to Jerusalem according to custom. The will of God was expressed for her through the Law, which applied to her entire people and to the entirety of their life together, as well as through the word that an angel spoke to her. Mary had learned to be obedient to God in part by conforming to the Law of Moses.

The first chapter of *Abandonment to Divine Providence*, by Jean Pierre de Caussade, contains an intriguing description of what it means to accept God's will in one's life:

> The duties of each moment are the shadows beneath which hides the divine operation. "The power of the Most High shall over-shadow thee" (*Lk* 1:35), said the angel to Mary. This shadow, beneath which is hidden the power of God for the purpose of bringing forth Jesus Christ in the soul, is the duty, the attraction, or the cross that is presented to us at each moment. These are, in

> fact, but shadows like those in the order of nature which, like a veil, cover sensible objects and hide them from us. Therefore in the moral and supernatural order the duties of each moment conceal, under the semblance of dark shadows, the truth of their divine character which alone should rivet the attention. It was in this light that Mary beheld them.

The purpose of the examen is to be able to recognise those times when the power of the Most High overshadows us, whether those occasions involve duties, attractions or crosses: so that Christ can be born in our hearts. If we can recognise that God has broken into our lives through the Mother of God, then we will find a way to recognise, and accept, what the Most High has in store for us.

I have the answer before my eyes

When one sees that duties, attractions and crosses are all an expression of the will of God, one comes to realise that God is the one who establishes what is truly real in life. St Maximilian, for instance, was convinced that it was Mary herself who shaped the events of his life, including his success in establishing the publishing empire. He once wrote:

> Sometimes I am amazed by the fact that, despite my great ignorance, the mistakes, the clumsiness, the weaknesses, and many, many other difficulties, Rycerz (the magazine called "Knight of the Immaculate") still exists and grows much more than other magazines. Sometimes it happens

> that I stop at the front door of the machine room and I wonder: "Where does this come from?" But as soon as I raise my head, I have the answer before my eyes: the Immaculata. She shows what she can do. The greater our inability and the more difficult the obstacles are to overcome, the more she shows that she does everything by herself. Recognising this is the source of the exceptional development potential of our publishing complex.[13]

One of the things that convinced St Maximilian that the Immaculata was at work in his life was noticing that he often received unexpected favours on Marian feast days. Everything that occurred on these days in particular was for him an opportunity to accept the will of the Mother of God, united as her will is with that of her Son. St Bernadette was similarly aware that Mary reached out to her on particular days. A fellow novice who had been sick and confined to the infirmary said that Bernadette had once told her:

> Rest easy, you'll be cured.... The Blessed Virgin doesn't want me to observe my month of Mary in the infirmary by myself. And here you are. We'll do it together. Let's pray hard to her and she will cure you.[14]

The novice recalled that together they had found ways to honour Mary during the month of May and that she had

---

[13] *Ibid.*, Letter 137.

[14] Fr Ren Laurentin, *Bernadette Speaks* (trans. J. Lynch and R. DesRosiers) (Pauline Books and Media, 2000) p. 451.

left the infirmary on 1st June. The saints took days that are associated with Mary as occasions to grow closer to her.

Fr Langford wrote that Mother Teresa came to see that Our Lady arranged for her the events that she encountered in life. In giving to Our Lady "repeatedly through the day and over the course of the years, our worries, doubts, pains, problems, and all self-reference",[15] Mother Teresa gave Our Lady full permission to act in her life.

You live in poverty, wanting nothing more

God is at work in our lives. It is in pondering on the events of life that one recognises this. We need help if we are to learn to reflect on our lives and to live in light of that reflection. The saints found that this was possible because they adopted a habitual practice or joined a group where others encouraged them to give expression to their love for Mary. The "Little Way" of St Thérèse of Lisieux is grounded in accepting what happens to us as it unfolds before us, and in responding with generosity. In her poem "Why I love you, O Mary!" she wrote:

> Mother full of grace, I know that in Nazareth
> You live in poverty, wanting nothing more.
> No rapture, miracle, or ecstasy
> Embellish your life, O Queen of the Elect!

Thérèse was content with finding God in the ordinary events

---

[15] Langford, p. 37.

of life, just as Mary had been. One senses this even when she simply looks into the lens of a camera.

Hearts that burn

One need not only honour Mary by saying prayers, asking for her assistance or following her example of pondering on the events of life. The staggering greatness of God's action in Mary's life calls for a response that takes in one's heart, as was evident with Elizabeth's cry at the Visitation. If I no longer live but Christ lives in me, what depth of love for Mary should be in place within my heart! Further indications of the depth of affection for Our Lady on the part of early Christians come from the fifth century. It is not possible to sing with a cold heart! Not long after the Council of Ephesus, the Jerusalem Church, as part of its Sunday liturgy, boasted a whole collection of hymns centred around the praise of the Virgin Mary, including the following lines in one hymn:

> You, the fleece of the holy rain from heaven,
> By whom the shepherd of the sheep was clothed,
> Handmaid and mother and virgin, heaven of the heavens,
> The only bridge for God's coming to humankind,
> Awesome loom of our economy,
> On which the garment of the Lord was ineffably woven,
> Pray for us, O holy Queen,
> Do not cease to intercede for the salvation of our souls.[16]

---

[16] Stephen Shoemaker, *Mary in Early Christian Faith and Devotion* (Yale University Press, 2016) p. 190.

QUE SOY
ERA
IMMACULADA COUNCEPCIOU

Separated from the grotto at Lourdes

A readiness to praise the glories of Mary from the depths of one's heart is a mark of the saints. When he was conversing with others, St John Eudes often kissed a medal of the rosary that he kept about himself. When asked why he did this, he would tell people that he kissed the medal out of love. In the eighteenth century, St Leonard of Port Maurice wore a medal of the Madonna on his breast, often pressing the medal to his heart or gazing at it. St John Vianney served as the parish priest for the village of Ars, France, for forty years during the nineteenth century. When he was a young lad, St John carried a little statue of Our Lady around with him, even taking it to bed. During the process for his canonisation, one villager testified that his face would light up with a smile whenever he turned to the statue of Our Lady in the parish church.

St Bernadette, meanwhile, was particularly attached to the grotto at Lourdes where Our Lady appeared to her, shown in the image left. She wept frequently during the first few days after arriving as a novice at the mother house of the Sisters of Charity in Nevers, France. One of the other novices assumed that she missed her family, but Bernadette told her that it was the separation from the grotto at Lourdes that pained her. She would forevermore have to accept that she could no longer visit it. In time, she found consolation in praying in the garden of the convent, before a statue of Our Lady of the Waters.

Why not find a way to become attached to sites that are associated with Mary, whether these are nearby or far away, following something of St Bernadette's path to sanctity? This could be made possible by occasionally booking time off work to celebrate a Marian feast day or by using some of your holidays to undertake pilgrimages.

Devoting oneself to prayer

The heart, though, is not just about one's affections. The word "heart" is used in the Bible to refer to the depths of a person's being, to the place where one makes decisions before God. It was Pharaoh's heart that hardened in refusing to let the people of Israel leave Egypt, and in Ezekiel 36 we hear that God will hallow his name by removing the hearts of stone from his people and giving them hearts of flesh instead. One particularly prevalent theme that is apparent in the lives of the saints is the way that an affection for Our Lady led them to extend their prayers. In this way, the saints made it clear that their lives in their entirety were to be given over to God.

The three seers of Fátima prayed the Rosary endlessly. Lúcia once recounted about herself and her two cousins:

> One day, we were playing on the stone slabs of the well down at the bottom of the garden belonging to my parents, which we called the Arneiro. Suddenly, we saw beside us the same figure, or rather Angel, as it seemed to me. "What are you doing?" he asked. "Pray, pray very much! The most holy Hearts of Jesus and Mary have

designs of mercy on you. Offer prayers and sacrifices constantly to the Most High."[17]

St John Vianney became famous for spending hour upon hour in the confessional, as much as sixteen hours a day during the summer months. As a child, John was a shepherd, responsible for looking after a small flock of sheep. He encouraged other children to say a single *Hail Mary* with him, whereas he was not content with saying only a single prayer. He himself prayed for hours on end before his beloved statue of Our Lady.

What is evident in the example of St John Vianney, the three seers of Fátima, and others is that Mary is a person whose company one keeps and who draws one closer to Christ. We hear that, prior to Pentecost day, the mother of Jesus spent time in the company of her family and all the brethren: "All these with one accord devoted themselves to prayer, together with the women and Mary the mother of Jesus, and with his brethren" (*Ac* 1:14). The Greek word for "devoted" here is more accurately translated as "continued steadfastly". It is no wonder that so many of the saints were led by Our Lady to extend their prayers, in a similar fashion to the apostles, the women and Jesus's other family members. By staying in prayer with Our Lady we prepare to receive the Holy Spirit. Our Lady's presence hailed the arrival of the Holy Spirit at Pentecost, just as her presence

---

[17] Kondor, p. 78.

hailed the arrival of Christ for Elizabeth, and as St John the Baptist was moved by the Spirit in his mother's womb.

Passing beads through his fingers

The Rosary especially offers us a way to spend extended time in prayer in the company of Our Lady. It typically takes twenty minutes or so to pray one set of mysteries, but why stop at praying just one set each day? Padre Pio prayed the Rosary whenever he had spare time. Rather than take a long siesta like his brother friars, he used most of that time to say the Rosary, often seated on a veranda in the friary. Whenever he was going from one place to another, he could be seen passing beads through his fingers. Why not find further time in the day when you are regularly able to pray the Rosary, for instance when walking, commuting or moving around the house? Why not keep a rosary in your pocket for this purpose?

An additional means by which many of the saints extended their prayers was by gazing at images or icons of Our Lady, as we have already seen with St Maximilian Kolbe raising his eyes to see her statue. St Gabriel of Our Lady of Sorrows, a member of the Passionist Order, died of tuberculosis aged twenty-four. He always lingered in prayer before any images of Our Lady that he encountered during the day, as Padre Pio did also. The Russian Orthodox mystic, Seraphim of Sarov, meanwhile, used to pray in front of an image of the Mother of God called "Tenderness". He prayed to the Trinity, but always in front of this icon that he kept with him in his forest hut. It was as if Mary were taking his prayers to the Father, Son and Spirit. It is said that Our Lady would often visit him in his monastic cell, speaking with him and at times healing him. On one occasion, Our Lady is said to have turned to the apostle John, who also appeared along with her, saying to him about Seraphim, "This is one of our line, of our race." An icon or painting of Our Lady should not simply be background art in one's home or place of work: it is something to be noticed whenever one is around it, something to remind us of our mother.

The third mansions and beyond

St Teresa of Avila indicated that praying for extended periods of time each day, even when prayer feels dry or difficult, is a core feature of what is required for spiritual growth. In the third mansions, souls come into their own in the spiritual life, trying to avoid even the slightest of sins, using their time for others – and, yes, giving hours of time to prayer. Even as a young boy, for instance, St Maximilian was frequently seen kneeling before the altar that his family had dedicated to Our Lady. Pope St Pius V spent many hours in prayer in his youth, watching over his father's sheep. He recited the Rosary repeatedly. Learning to be faithful to praying the Rosary helps to make a life of charity possible, as Mother Teresa was keenly aware. In explaining the original constitutions of the Missionaries of Charity, she indicated:

> We are taught to love and say the Rosary with great devotion; let us be very faithful to this our first love – for it will bring us closer to our Heavenly Mother. Our rule asks of us never to go to the slums without first having recited the Mother's praises; that is why we have to say the Rosary in the streets and dark holes of the slums. Cling to the Rosary as the creeper clings to the tree – for without Our Lady we cannot stand.[18]

Growth in prayer beyond the third mansions, meanwhile, begins to touch on something beyond the length of time for which one prays. Prayer in the fourth mansions is characterised by an experience of recollection in which a person closes his or her eyes and builds a space in the soul within which to be aware of God. A state of absorption is present in one's will that comes as a gift from God. One finds that attempts at an active use of the understanding become impossible, so that prayer is characterised by silence and wonder. This experience of prayer is one that St Thérèse knew well. At one point she said, "And I cannot pray. I can only look at Our Blessed Lady and say: 'Jesus!'" Earlier, in writing the *Story of a Soul*, she observed:

> With me prayer is an uplifting of the heart; a glance towards heaven; a cry of gratitude and love, uttered equally in sorrow and in joy. In a word, it is something noble, supernatural, which expands my soul and unites it

[18] Kolodiejchuk, p. 141.

to God. Sometimes when I am in such a state of spiritual dryness that not a single good thought occurs to me, I say very slowly the "Our Father" or the "Hail Mary", and these prayers suffice to take me out of myself, and wonderfully refresh me.

It is clear in the Gospel of Luke that Mary's own prayer went beyond words and images, given the emphasis on her heart. A sense of wonder within her soul and her spirit at the action of God, meanwhile, comes across as a dominant thread in the *Magnificat*. Luke subsequently indicates that all who heard the shepherds' account of the message of the angel that a saviour had been born that day wondered at what the shepherds told them (*Lk* 2:18). This included Mary herself. Luke specifically observed that Mary marvelled at the words of Simeon (*Lk* 2:33). To wonder is a form of prayer, involving, as it does, both silence and contemplation.

Nourished in the wilderness

While St Teresa indicated that few Christian souls reach the fifth mansions, it is still helpful to appreciate how Our Lady acts as a mother who brings her children to maturity. The fifth mansions are marked out by the prayer of union, in which the body (and the distractions that come with it) truly seems remote from the soul. St Teresa indicated that, after an occasion of the prayer of union, one is convinced that God has been in the soul and the soul has been in God. Such prayer is only possible if the soul has entirely surrendered itself to God. We have already seen the evident way in which Mary accepted God's will for herself across her life. The absence of distractions, though, is something that is specifically apparent in Mary's life of prayer. Revelation 12 indicates that, after the woman had given birth to a male child, she fled away from the serpent into the wilderness, where she had a place prepared by God. There she was nourished for 1,260 days – "for a time, and times, and half a time" (*Rv* 12:14).

In the Old Testament, the wilderness was a place of encounter with God beyond all diversions. It was in the wilderness, for instance, that Moses encountered the Lord in the burning bush and that Elijah met God in the sound of a low whisper outside the cave. Mary's prayer occurred as if she were permanently in the desert, where she was nourished for a truly extended period on every word that proceeds from the mouth of God. If we want to encounter God in the deepest forms of prayer, then the teaching of St Teresa's fellow-traveller on the paths of prayer, St John of the Cross, would point us towards prayer that is undertaken away from all the satisfactions of this world. To enter into the depths of prayer, St John of the Cross recommended "complete detachment and emptiness and poverty, with respect to everything that is in the world, for Christ's sake".

A union of hearts

According to St Teresa, the sixth mansions are characterised by a time of trial and of awakenings, during which God moves the soul to its utter depths. The saints particularly turned to Our Lady for assistance in living through trials. For instance, St Bernadette once told a friend that she was tortured by interior distress. As time wore on, she had to face a failing memory as to the events of the apparitions at Lourdes. Various histories of the events were conflicting, and she suffered from the animosities between the parties involved. She also had a fear that she had not lived up to the graces that she received. Even still, she turned to Our Lady for assistance. After all, Our Lady had said to Bernadette during the first apparition, "I do not promise to make you happy in this world, but in the next." Our Lady was close to St Bernadette in all her trials, in part through Bernadette's memory of these words.

The sixth mansions are also marked out by an awareness of one's union with God that is continuous. According to Fr Emile Neubert in *Life of Union with Mary*, for some saints this awareness of God was accompanied by an experience of Mary's presence as well. It would seem that this was true for St Bernard of Clairvaux in the twelfth century, given that he may have spoken from personal experience in saying, "May she not leave our mind; may she not leave our tongue." A priest once asked Padre Pio if the Blessed Virgin ever visited him in his cell. His response was to say,

"You should ask rather if she is ever absent from my cell." As he once told a canon from the cathedral in Rouen, St Louis-Marie de Montfort had an abiding awareness of the presence of both Jesus and Mary in the depths of his heart. This awareness helped him to live through the trials that he experienced as a wandering missionary, subject as he was to the misunderstandings and animosity of many of the priests and bishops he encountered.

There is no tension at all between the presence of Christ and the presence of his mother. St Maximilian once wrote to a fellow Franciscan friar who had questioned how it was possible to love both Jesus and Mary at the same time, "But were you able to love together your father and your mother and also your brothers and sisters?"[19]

The heights of prayer and holiness

It is evident that Mary accompanies the soul at every stage of this journey into maturity, into the innermost mansions of the interior castle. We can be confident that Mary is our mother because she leads us ever closer to Christ. By matching the teaching of St Teresa of Avila with the way that the saints related to Mary, we have seen a series of staging points on the path to sanctity. St Teresa's book, *The Interior Castle*, is like a developmental chart that maps out the stages of growth in the spiritual life, from the starkness of baptism to the graces of the seventh mansions. In this

[19] Kolbe, Letter 643.

developmental process, one becomes ever more closely conformed to the model of prayer and life that Our Lady exhibited. Devotion to Our Lady leads directly to growth in the depth of one's prayer, and to ever-greater holiness. One cannot manufacture on demand a life that is close to Christ. Where else do you see such an array of those who have reached the heights of prayer and holiness, other than in the Catholic Church? And when you see signs in your life that Mary is a spiritual mother who has given birth to you and who cares for you, then what else can you do but abandon yourself into her arms?

Conceived without sin

The growth in prayer that St Teresa describes is only possible for us when accompanied by a conversion of one's entire life. At the same time, it is fascinating that no path of conversion is evident in the accounts of Mary's life in the Gospels. None of the Gospel incidents in which she figures offer even the slightest hint that she herself needed to convert. This is clearly not an accident. Even John the Baptist, of whom Christ said there was none greater born amongst men, required a conversion, sending word as he did to Jesus, "Are you the one who is to come, or shall we look for another?" (*Mt* 11:3). As the Second Eve, Our Lady was without sin, just as Adam's wife, Eve, is portrayed as being without sin prior to the Fall. The text in Genesis indicates that the man and his wife "were both naked and were not ashamed" (2:25). Pope St John Paul II taught in his theology of the body that Adam and Eve were graced with an original innocence prior to eating the apple. Given the teaching that Mary is the Second Eve, the entire corpus of John Paul's theology of the body – focused as it is on expounding on what life was like in the beginning before sin entered the world – is a testament to the truth that Mary was conceived without sin.

It did not take long for the teaching that Mary is the Second Eve to find a grip across the entire Church. Saint John Henry Newman pointed out that, by the year 200, Fathers of the Church in as diverse settings as Africa, Rome, Palestine, Asia Minor and Gaul were comparing Mary to Eve. For instance, Justin Martyr wrote around the year 150 that Eve brought forth disobedience and death, while Mary received the word of the angel with joy and faith, bringing forth the Son of God. St John had died around twenty years before St Justin's conversion. St Irenaeus, meanwhile, taught that "the knot of the disobedience of Eve was untied through the obedience of Mary". St Irenaeus was a disciple of Polycarp, who had in his turn been a follower of St John. Under the title of the Second Eve, Mary is acknowledged as the mother of all those who are alive in Christ, of all those who keep the commandments of God and hold to the testimony of Jesus. Her son is the firstborn of many brothers (*Rm* 8:29).

The recollections, autobiographies, letters, poems and prayers of the saints indicate a clear role for Our Lady in personally helping them to come alive in Christ. This pertains to what Fr Aidan Nichols in *There Is No Rose* has called subjective redemption. It pertains to the communication to the faithful of the fruits of Christ's incarnation and his death on the cross. Mary takes care of all her children and leads them to a life that is genuinely close to Christ.

Taking her to our own

Commentators have identified a pattern that recurs several times in John's Gospel. Two people are mentioned, a protagonist sees someone and says "Behold", and then the protagonist reveals something profound about the other person, giving that person a title. For instance, Jesus saw Nathanael coming to him and said, "Behold, an Israelite indeed, in whom is no guile!" (*Jn* 1:47). This pattern is also evident in the scene at the foot of the cross that we reflected upon at the beginning of the book. Furthermore, in both this incident with Nathaniel and the scene at the cross, Jesus's action was designed to call forth a response on the part of the other person. Nathaniel professed his belief in Christ as the Son of God and the King of Israel. What response occurred after Christ said to the beloved disciple, "Behold, your mother"?

John's Gospel states that, after Jesus entrusted the beloved disciple to his mother and his mother to the disciple, the disciple took Mary to his own home. Pope Benedict XVI pointed out that the Greek phrase for "took her to his own home" translates literally as "welcomed her into his own existence". It is as if the lives of the woman and the disciple are joined together. Immediately after this, the Gospel goes on to state that Jesus knew that "all was now finished" (*Jn* 19:28). This mutual entrustment between mother and disciple completed the work that his Father had given to Jesus. It is no wonder that Pope Benedict concluded during a sermon on the Solemnity of Mary, Mother of God:

> Therefore, at the supreme moment of the fulfilment of his messianic mission, Jesus bequeaths as a precious inheritance to each one of his disciples his own Mother, the Virgin Mary.

Entering into a pact with the *Immaculata*

One way or another, the saints all came to appreciate Mary as their mother in the most heartfelt of ways. We have seen that some of the saints experienced this early in life, as with St Thérèse of Lisieux, St Catherine Labouré or the seers of Fátima. St Teresa of Avila's mother died when Teresa was about twelve years old. St Teresa recounted in her *Life*:

> When I began to realise what I had lost, I went in distress to an image of Our Lady and with many tears besought her to be a mother to me. Though I did this in my simplicity, I believe it was of some avail to me; for whenever I have commended myself to this Sovereign Virgin I have been conscious of her aid; and eventually she has brought me back to herself.

For other saints, though, this appreciation came into its own as they reached maturity. It was given expression through a formal act of consecration to Mary. It was when he was a young man that Pope St John Paul II first read St Louis-Marie de Montfort's book *True Devotion to the Blessed Virgin*. At the time, Karol was working as a forced labourer in a quarry and chemical plant. Louis-Marie had advocated a thirty-three-day period of prayer to prepare oneself for a consecration to Jesus through Mary. Karol undertook this consecration. He became so attached to his copy of the book that he carried it with him wherever he went. It soon became stained with lime from the chemical plant. Pope St John Paul later recalled:

> During the Second World War, while I was employed as a factory worker, I came to be attracted to Marian devotion. At first, it had seemed to me that I should distance myself a bit from the Marian devotion of my childhood, in order to focus more on Christ. Thanks to Saint Louis of Montfort, I came to understand that true devotion to the Mother of God is actually Christocentric, indeed, it is very profoundly rooted in the Mystery of the Blessed Trinity, and the mysteries of the Incarnation and Redemption.

A path of affection, devotion and even friendship with Our Lady is required for one to be drawn deeply into the interpersonal life of the Trinity. Based on her own experience, Mother Teresa highlighted just one thing when she asked her sisters to entrust themselves entirely to Mary:

> We need to spend personal time each day with Our Lady. This means dedicating some moments, no matter how brief, to conscious contact with her.... The length of time given to our visits with Our Lady is not as important as their frequency and constancy.[20]

St Maximilian's approach was similarly simple: "To enter into a pact with the Immaculata, no formula is required. Simply say to her, like a child to its mother, that you are making such an agreement." A willingness to dedicate their lives to their mother, the Blessed Virgin Mary, is a truly insistent theme in the lives of the saints. If you have not already entered into a pact with Mary, your mother, then why not decide to do so? And then renew this pact by consciously turning to Our Lady in one way or other each day that follows, freely speaking to her from the depths of your heart.

Too much love?

If there is a need for each individual Christian to take Our Lady to his or her own, there is also a need for a renewed appreciation of what it means for Mary's role as a mother across the entire life of the Church. It is sadly the case that after the Second Vatican Council a winter descended upon devotion to Our Lady. The Council text *Lumen Gentium*

---

[20] Langford, p. 77.

exhorted theologians and preachers to "abstain zealously both from all gross exaggerations as well as from petty narrow-mindedness in considering the singular dignity of the Mother of God." How easy is it, though, to abstain "zealously" from gross exaggerations without giving up on devotion? The Council Fathers also cautioned the faithful to remember that true devotion to Mary does not consist in either "sterile or transitory affection". A commentator has pointed out that *Lumen Gentium* is decidedly defensive when discussing Mary's role as our mother, making use of nine negatives in the space of three short paragraphs.[21] St Maximilian Kolbe had wisdom that was sorely called for at the Council: "Never be afraid of loving the Blessed Virgin too much. You can never love her more than Jesus did."

The notion that one can never fully sing Mary's praises is a refrain of the saints across the ages. We hear Origen embellishing the words of Elizabeth in order to refer to Mary as "my Lady": "It is I who should have come to visit you, because you are blessed above all women, you are the Mother of my Lord, you are my Lady." In his sermon on the Feast of the Purification, Bishop Methodius in the early fourth century recognised that he struggled to give Mary her due, in that the "remembrance of this holy virgin far transcends all words of mine". The first ever complete biography of Mary, *The Life of the Virgin*, was probably

[21] Charles W. Neumann, "Mary and the Church: Lumen Gentium, Arts. 60 to 65", Marian Studies 37(12) 1986.

written by St Maximus the Confessor in the seventh century. It starts out: "The praise and glory, laud and honour of our all-holy, incorruptible, and most blessed queen, the Theotokos and ever-virgin Mary." One can hear the way in which he struggled to find words that do justice to the Mother of God.

Pope Benedict XVI went as far as to say in his book *Mary: The Church at the Source* that an "immediate outcome" of the Second Vatican Council text *Lumen Gentium* was the "collapse" of the theological study of Mary. He linked this collapse to the inclusion in the text of a way of understanding Mary's role in the Church that was, at least partly, impersonal. He argued that this had a significant impact on the Church, directly linking it to the subsequent concentration of religious feeling in Latin America on political change. He commented, "In theology it is not the person that is reducible to the thing, but the thing to the person." It seems to me that winter has not yet entirely given way to spring.

A "Little Way" for the Church

The Church needs renewed forms of Marian devotion if the faithful are to receive the graces God has prepared for us. Pope Benedict went on to write, "Only the Marian dimension secures the place of affectivity in faith and thus ensures a fully human correspondence to the reality of the incarnate Logos." A Marian dimension is not an option for the Church, but a necessity.

A suitable affectivity, for instance, is desperately necessary in relation to participation in the Church's liturgy, at least if the value of meditation and contemplation is to become suitably apparent in this setting. The Second Vatican Council's Constitution on the Sacred Liturgy, *Sacrosanctum Concilium*, acknowledged that, "other things being equal", Gregorian chant "should be given pride of place in liturgical services" (116). One of the main reasons why Gregorian chant is particularly suited to the Roman liturgy is that it supports meditation and contemplation on the part of both singers and listeners. For instance, each word of a melismatic chant, in which almost every syllable is provided with many notes, is given due time for its meaning to strike home and for beauty to still the heart. Unfortunately, what happened with the liturgical reform was that Gregorian chant was all but abandoned across the Church in favour of bodies of music in the vernacular that have to all intents and purposes been instantly fabricated. A rediscovery of Gregorian chant would be Marian in its orientation, in recognising the centrality of contemplation in liturgical life.

And if theological study of Mary suffered after the Council, so too did the willingness of Catholics to join with each other in their devotion to Our Lady, lest they be led astray. What a need there is in the Church of today for Christians to connect to each other in their love for Our Lady! Every single family, association, order or movement in the Church that has not yet dedicated itself to Our

Lady should consecrate itself to her. Just as the Trinity incorporates within it interpersonal relations, so Christianity is a companionship and not simply a set of practices and ideas. This companionship includes not only those fellow Christians who live alongside us, but also angels, saints and Our Lady, as well as the Holy Trinity.

And what of the implications for Christians at large? When framing its teaching on Our Lady, Vatican II placed significant emphasis on taking account of Protestant sensibilities, cautioning preachers and teachers to "assiduously keep away from whatever, either by word or deed, could lead separated brethren or any other into error regarding the true doctrine of the Church". What is really needed, though, is for our separated brothers and sisters to be drawn towards a greater affection for their spiritual mother who will be able to assist their conversion. Attempts to restore unity amongst all Christians should not be dissolved into an impersonal spiritual journey. St Thérèse of Lisieux was clear that God is the one who does the heavy lifting, just as she knew that Mary was the one who helped prepare her to encounter God. It is hard to see any path to the restoration of unity among all Christ's followers other than a Marian one.

A transformative grace

This book has sought to open a window onto the personal relationship that each Christian has with his or her spiritual mother by looking, as it were, through the hearts of saints. What have we seen during the attempt?

In a homily for the Feast of the Assumption, Pope Benedict XVI observed that Mary has been taken up into heaven. Even still, Mary is close to us because "she is with God and in God". She could only be close to a few people while on earth, but because God is close to us, she is now close to all of us as well. We have seen across this book that the saints experienced being close to both the Mother of God and Jesus at the same time, whether by meditating on the action of God, by calling out in times of need and receiving an answer, or by following her example. Mary is someone who is present to her children as a companion. One of the reasons that this book has given extended attention to apparitions of Our Lady is that the associated stories bring into sharp relief the truth that Mary is a living being who loves specific people. Christians do not live autonomous lives, detached from their mother. As we saw at the start of this book with Lúcia, Francisco and Jacinta, an appreciation that Mary is a living person leads one to realise that Christ, too, is alive and longing for our companionship.

God ordained that Jesus's mother should have a key role to play in the growth to maturity of all Christians. The thirteenth- to fourteenth-century poet Dante had St Bernard of Clairvaux say in the *Divine Comedy*: "Lady, thou art so great and so powerful, that whoever desires grace yet does not turn to thee, would have his desire fly

without wings." The certainty of the saints that Mary is the mother of all Christians stems from her initiative in their lives, and from their recognition of that initiative. The saints found many ways to honour Our Lady in their daily lives, to call her blessed and to reach out to her with affection. In this way, each of the saints welcomed Mary into his or her own existence. Each follower of Christ should find ways to receive her as a beloved mother. Growth in holiness does not stem, in the first instance, from our own effort or planning; it comes as a gift to us through the hands of our mother.

At the foot of the cross

God can work great things from seemingly small beginnings. Calling the Mother of God "blessed" opens up many possibilities - whether a readiness to seek her help, an appreciation of the way that God overshadows one's life, or growth in prayer - so that we can come to share in the transformation of grace that she received.

In Masaccio's fresco *Holy Trinity*, Mary looks out towards the viewer. The look is one of deep sorrow, suggesting that the eyes of her heart remain fixed on God. John's gaze in turn seems partly directed at Mary, as well as given over to prayer. He accepts Christ's gift. The beloved disciple took Mary to his own home in response to Christ's words. Even now Christ says to us, "Behold, your mother."

The *Memorare*

Remember, O most loving Virgin Mary, that it is a thing unheard of, that anyone ever had recourse to your protection, implored your help, or sought your intercession, and was left forsaken. Filled therefore with confidence in your goodness I fly to you, O Mother, Virgin of virgins. To you I come, before you I stand, a sorrowful sinner. Despise not my poor words, O Mother of the Word of God, but graciously hear and grant my prayer.

Image Credits

Cover: *Madonna della Misericordia* (*Madonna of Mercy*), c.1527 by Vincenzo Tamagni. Found in the collection of Museo Civico e Diocesano d'Arte Sacra. Heritage Images / Fine Art Images / akg-images.

Page 6: *The Assumption of the Virgin* c. 1500 by Michel Sittow. Ailsa Mellon Bruce Fund, National Gallery of Art, Washington, D.C.

Page 12: *Lúcia Santos, Jacinta and Francisco Marto*, 1917, photo by Joshua Benoliel © Shrine of Fatima.

Pages 18 and 89: *Holy Trinity*, 1425–1427, Santa Maria Novella, Florence, Italy by Tommaso Masaccio. Public domain, via Wikimedia Commons.

Page 27: *Our Lady of Guadalupe*, 1531, Basilica of Guadalupe, Mexico City. Wikicommons.

Page 33: *Pontefract Castle*, Pontefract, England by Alexander Keirincx, public domain, via Wikimedia Commons.

Page 44: *Our Lady of the Rosary*, Shrine of Fatima, Portugal. Ricardo Perna / Shutterstock.com.

Page 57: *Book of Kells. Folio 7v: Virgin and Child*, Trinity College Dublin, Ireland. © The Board of Trinity College Dublin.

Page 66: Grotto of Lourdes, France. LorenzoPeg / Shutterstock.com.

page 92: *The Immaculate Conception*, 1830, by Philip Veit, The Church of Trinità Dei Monti, Rome, Italy. Renata Sedmakova / Shutterstock.com.